READING
OLD & NEW

TEXT & INTRODUCTION
DAPHNE PHILLIPS

NEW PHOTOGRAPHS BY
READING CHRONICLE

PUBLISHED JOINTLY BY
COUNTRYSIDE BOOKS & READING CHRONICLE

First Published 1986
© Text Daphne Phillips 1986

All rights reserved. No reproduction permitted without the
prior permission of the publishers:

COUNTRYSIDE BOOKS
3 CATHERINE ROAD
NEWBURY, BERKSHIRE

ISBN 0 905392 73 6

Produced through MRM (Print Consultants) Ltd, Reading
Typeset by Acorn Bookwork, Salisbury
Printed and bound in England by Borcombe Printers, Romsey

INTRODUCTION

A town like Reading, adaptable to changes in industry, commerce and communications, is forever casting off the old to make way for the new. Space is at a premium, so there is never a time when several town centre sites are not concealed behind scaffolding, to emerge months later in a different guise. This piecemeal process has been going on for generations, but in recent years comprehensive redevelopments have swept away large numbers of buildings in one fell swoop.

This book can only show a few of the changes which have taken place in the last 100 years. Some of the photographs will remind older residents of familiar street scenes, shops and houses which once seemed an integral part of daily life, permanent and unchanging. Yet those buildings, now demolished, may themselves have enjoyed comparatively short lives, having replaced ones familiar to a previous age. Other photographs record buildings which have played major roles in the history of Reading – the Abbey, the three ancient parish churches, the old Town Hall, the former coaching inns. All of these have been so changed by time that they can now give only a hint of what they looked like in the past, being little more than proof that history really happened. The ragged remains of Reading Abbey, even with the restored inner gateway and hospitium, demand a considerable effort of imagination to be seen as one of the wealthiest abbeys in the land, where kings, prelates and parliaments were entertained, and which dominated this town from the 12th to the 16th century. The churches of St Mary, St Laurence and St Giles, more adaptable to change, have survived although greatly altered, just as the old Town Hall, the seat of municipal government for 400 years, was enlarged and rebuilt more than once before the council migrated to larger offices on the other side of town.

Changes in industry and modes of transport have left their mark on Reading. Waterborne traffic was important from earliest times to a town built near the confluence of the Thames and the Kennet, and its wharfs were even busier in the 18th and 19th centuries when the great canal was constructed linking the Kennet with the Avon and the west country. Sadly, pictures of working barges on the canal are rare, but the wharfs remain, deserted now and peaceful compared with the noisy streets a short distance away. Reading has always been situated on important roads. In particular the great London to Bath and Bristol road passing through it dictated the position of many of the inns which flourished here in coaching days. Few of these have survived but this book includes two – the Sun and the Ship. The other inn shown, the Great Western Hotel, was not built until after the railway was opened and the years of its prosperity were years of decline for the coaching inns.

Railways not only revolutionised transport but made possible the rapid expansion of the town's leading industries: Simond's beer, Sutton's seeds and Huntley & Palmer's biscuits. Each of these required extensive works and offices near the town centre which they occupied for well over a century. It is only in recent years that these great establishments, with which Reading was identified, have moved away, leaving their sites to be cleared for redevelopment. Another local industry whose products can still be seen all over Reading was that of brickmaking. Collier's, Poulton's and Wheeler's kilns have long been closed but dozens of streets and houses built in pleasing patterns of red, cream and grey bricks, bear witness to the vitality of local craftsmanship.

Within living memory horsedrawn vehicles have disappeared from the streets; and gone, too, are the trams and trolleybuses so affectionately remembered. In the last 30 years motor vehicles have radically changed the appearance of the town, not only by the demolition of buildings for road widening, the construction of car parks, roundabouts, islands, traffic signs and pedestrian crossings, but by the ceaseless tide of vehicles moving through the streets, and pausing only to fume impatiently at traffic lights.

Photographs past and present show other ways in which the town has changed. There are differences in textures and materials as well as in the scale and style of buildings. Patterned brick and terra-cotta flowers and finials have given way to plain brickwork, plain concrete and towering walls of glass. So often a whole row of small, homely shops, houses, pubs and cafes of various dates, heights and styles has been replaced by a single department store or office block, sometimes so huge and overpowering that people using it appear like ants. Certainly modern materials and design make parts of the town look brighter and shinier now, and it is probably more colourful; for it cannot be denied that in the older photographs many buildings look shabby and badly in need of a coat of paint. But, in spite of the dinginess and the liberal spatterings of horse manure on the dusty roads, there was a noticeable lack of litter. It seems that takeaway foods and the packaging industry have also left their marks on Reading.

Older Readingensians remember when country walks through fields and copses were within easy reach of the town centre, and the river banks were in their natural state. The farmlands which then encircled Reading have gradually been sold and covered with housing or industrial estates. Historic houses, such as Southcote Manor and Caversham Court have been demolished, and ugly industrialisation allowed to ruin much of the river scenery. Luckily the recreational potential of Reading's waterways has now been recognised and a network of pleasant riverside walks away from the hectic streets is being developed.

Last but not least of the differences between old and new are the changes in the appearance of the people, to whom photographs owe so much of their sense of time, occasion and mood. Today's casual styles are as expressive as the formal modes of earlier periods. May all those people who kindly, if unknowingly, played a part in the 1986 photographs find a special pleasure in this book, for just as powerfully as remembered streets and buildings, they will remind us of the way we were.

Daphne Phillips

CONTENTS

BROAD STREET c. 1897

CIRCUS ELEPHANTS parade through the town, and behind them can be seen several carriers' carts, including Hawkins' and Withers' which served the Swallowfield area. On the site of the old brick houses the Vaudeville Cinema was opened in 1909.

BROAD STREET 1986

THE CINEMA was replaced by Timothy Whites (now Boots) in 1957. To the right of that in 1897 was Dowsett's Brewery retail department, where Dolcis now stands. The Duke's Head was partly replaced about 1933 by Lyons restaurant which closed in 1969 and is now Etam's.

THE OPPOSITE SIDE of Broad Street during the celebrations for the coronation of George VI on 12 May 1937. Just passing is the Cooperative Society's float advertising summer sportswear. In the background is Boots first big store in Broad Street established c. 1910.

BROAD STREET 1986

THE UPPER FLOORS of all the buildings, including the Broad Street Independent Chapel (now closed) next to Boots, have hardly changed but all the shopfronts at street level have been modernised. The Granada shop, which is dated 1898, was Baylis the grocers in 1937.

CHAIN STREET CORNER c. 1902

FORMERLY THE Post Office Tavern, 96 Broad Street became Poynder's Post Office Bookshop and Library in 1900. A selection of books at a penny each was displayed outside. Standing beside his iron bin (left) is a street orderly, better known as a dung boy, in his uniform and pillbox hat.

CHAIN STREET CORNER 1986

SILVER'S TOOK over Poynder's in 1919. Gaetano Borelli's was taken over by Samuels in 1906 and is now Wallis Fashions. The G.P.O. was on the opposite corner (now Topshop) until it moved to its present Friar Street site in 1924.

BROAD STREET c. 1905

LOOKING TOWARDS King Street in the early years of electric tramways. Passengers board a Wokingham Road tram (left) while old-fashioned modes of transport stand empty beneath the lofty tram standards. Buildings replaced by Marks & Spencer included the old Royal Oak and the Victoria Cafe run by H. A. Percy.

BROAD STREET 1986

ON THE RIGHT in 1905 the Angel, replaced by British Home Stores, and the Berks Training College of Music which occupied premises over Brain's boot and shoemaker's shop from 1903–26. The latter has survived as the K Shoe Shop.

DUKE STREET c. 1910

THE SHIP HOTEL, showing the old inn as it used to look in coaching days. A faded board claims that it is still a Commercial and Family Hotel but there is little sign of business. To the right, Brigham's well-stocked tobacconist's window suggests a brisker trade, while large signs appeal to customers to Smoke Tony Lumpkin.

DUKE STREET 1986

IT WAS the Ship, however, which survived and extended into Brigham's premises. Rebuilt in 1912 the front of the hotel now has a festive appearance with gilded swags and garlands over the windows.

MARKET PLACE c. 1890

THE DUSTY white road surface and ladies in frilled white blouses indicate a hot summer day. On the left the old timber-framed buildings, including Arthur Cooper's wine shop and Walter Wilson's estate agency (now Parker's), lean out towards the street. On the right, vertical lines have been achieved in brick and stone. Frank Cooksey's, auctioneer and estate agent, contrasts with the exuberant chequered brick of the Elephant Hotel next door.

MARKET PLACE 1986

IN THE 1970s the Market Place underwent extensive restyling. Some of the new arcaded shops can be seen on the right. Fortunately many of the other old buildings have been preserved, although The Coopers has been altered.

THE TOWN HALL 1953

ACCORDING to the clock it is not yet midnight but there is not a soul in sight to enjoy the decorations and the floodlighting in honour of the coronation of Elizabeth II. Only the marble statue of her great-great grandmother looks across at the shining portrait of the new Queen.

THE OLD TOWN HALL 1986

ALAS, the Town Hall designed by Alfred Waterhouse in 1872–5, is now the Old Town Hall and in a sorry state as it undergoes extensive refurbishment for other uses. Reading Borough Council moved to new Civic Offices in 1976.

ST LAURENCE'S CHURCH c. 1880

ONE OF THE three original parish churches of Reading, founded in the 12th century. Elizabeth I attended services here. Facing it can be seen the ancient Catherine Wheel Inn, demolished in 1882. Victorian developers replaced it and the adjoining buildings with new shops and offices.

ST LAURENCE'S CHURCH 1986

AN AIR RAID in 1943 badly damaged the church and all the buildings opposite. Bristol & West House, seen in the new picture, and the adjoining arcade were opened in 1957.

THE FORMER abbey hospitium (left) with the former St Laurence's Vicarage adjoining it when they housed Reading University Extension College, founded in 1892. The hospitium had been drastically restored for the use of the college. The tall building on the right was added to accommodate the British Dairy Institute, transferred from Aylesbury in 1896.

IN 1912, after the college had moved to London Road, the Institute building became the Borough Police Station. The others were occupied by council offices overflowing from the Town Hall. Only the hospitium now survives; a rather quaint adjunct to the imposing Guardian Royal Exchange Assurance Company offices.

BEYOND THE inner gateway of Reading Abbey, restored in 1861, stood a sedate row of houses in a quiet cul-de-sac appropriately named Abbot's Walk. They were built in the 1840s and 50s as private residences but many ended their days as temporary offices belonging to Berkshire County Council which, like the Borough Council, was suffering from a severe shortage of accommodation.

NOW THAT the County Council has moved to new Shire Hall this area is being redeveloped and the quiet cul-de-sac is used as a car park.

ABBOT'S WALK c. 1920

A VIEW from the eastern end looking towards St Laurence's. The house on the left became the Queen Victoria Institute for Nursing the Sick Poor of Reading in 1906. Later it was renamed the Queen Victoria Institute for District Nursing, but closed about 1938.

THE TWO end houses have recently been handsomely restored but all those between them and the Abbey Gateway have been demolished for some years and the site is to be part of a giant office development

THE FORBURY c. 1880

NUMBER 22 The Forbury was a fine late 17th century house, a reminder of the time when Reading was a small market town where people could live in pleasant surroundings within a short distance of the centre. Yet even by the 1880s industrial development in the shape of Sutton's Royal Seed Establishment had taken over the surrounding land, and the top of the huge seed stores can be glimpsed through the trees on the right.

THE FORBURY 1986

IN SPITE of a public protest which led to the formation of Reading Civic Society, 22 The Forbury was demolished in 1962 and one wing of the Prudential Assurance Company's offices now stands on the site.

FORBURY ROAD 1929

SEVERE WINTER weather has always caused transport problems but whereas the modern motorist depends on antifreeze this driver had to break the ice to enable his horse to drink. Small wonder that the horse is looking askance at the offered refreshment. The trough was one of many put up by the Drinking Fountain and Cattle Trough Association whose offices were in London.

FORBURY ROAD 1986

IN THE BACKGROUND on the old photograph, left, was the Police Station and, right, Petty's Printing Works (formerly the Queen's Hall). Guardian Royal Exchange and government offices now occupy the corners of Valpy Street.

ABBEY MILL c. 1960

ONE OF THE most important working buildings in Reading is seen at the end of its life. This flour mill, run by the Soundy family from the mid 19th century, had grown out of the original Reading Abbey mill established in the 12th century.

WHEN THE previous photograph was taken, the mill had been sold as 'Commodious warehouse premises', but it was doomed to be demolished and replaced by Berkshire County Council offices named Abbey Mill House.

ABBEY MILL 1964

THE ABBEY MILL during demolition showing, on the left behind the truck loaded with rubble, two waterwheels, and next to them the remains of two Norman arches across the Holy Brook. Also in the picture are the backs of Kings Road Baptist Church, demolished in 1985, and Cock's Reading Sauce factory.

34

ABBEY MILL ARCHES 1986

THE ARCHES have been preserved behind Abbey Mill House. The sauce factory has been replaced by the offices of International Business Machines. Part of the new Reading Central Library can be seen in the distance.

IN JUNE 1921 Reading staged a major historical pageant to mark the 800th anniversary of the founding of the great abbey by Henry I in 1121. Here a group of 'monks' sings the famous roundel 'Sumer is icumen in, Llude sing cuccu . . .' believed to have been first written down at this abbey in the 13th century.

READING ABBEY RUINS 1986

TODAY THE ruined walls of the Chapter House and Reredorter have been stripped of ivy, and all the remaining walls are undergoing a major restoration programme launched in 1984.

THE FORBURY LION c. 1888

THIS MEMORIAL was put up in 1886 as a tribute to the valour of the 66th Royal Berkshire Regiment at the Battle of Maiwand during the Afghan Campaign of 1880. For many years afterwards, on the anniversary of the battle, the monument was decorated with garlands of leaves, as seen here, by the surviving comrades and friends of the 328 officers and men who died.

THE FORBURY LION 1986

THE LION IS supported on four brick piers, one beneath each foot, concealed inside the pedestal which was originally faced with terra-cotta. As this did not wear well, it was refaced in stone in 1910.

THE KENNET 1929

DURING THE bitter weather of February 1929 the rivers froze over. Here a tug named Swan is seen towing barges through the icebound Kennet. The photograph was taken from the end of Crane Wharf, and on the right across the river can be seen part of Messer's timber yard.

THE KENNET 1986

MANY OF the houses in the centre of the earlier picture are still there but those far left have been replaced by new housing developments. Queens Road car park now fills the site of Messer's timber yard.

FRIAR STREET 1901

A SOLEMN OCCASION on 26 January 1901. The 63 year reign of Queen Victoria is over and, at the foot of her statue, the Town Clerk reads the proclamation of the accession of Edward VII in the presence of the Mayor and town council. Men of the local regiment, police and fire brigade line the street, while behind them hushed crowds watch and listen.

FRIAR STREET 1986

QUEEN VICTORIA'S STATUE, erected for her Golden Jubilee in 1887, has been enhanced by a paved pedestrian area planted with trees outside the Old Town Hall.

FRIAR STREET c. 1905

THE POPULAR Royal County Theatre, opened in 1895, is shown with posters advertising a drama entitled 'A Mother's Love'. On the left was a temperance hotel and, on the right, the tall building was Fidler's Seed Establishment. Outside the theatre stands one of Chaplin & Co's carriers vans.

FRIAR STREET 1986

THE THEATRE was destroyed by fire in 1937 and never rebuilt. Decorative Victorian has given way to utilitarian modern for Littlewoods, Shalets and Woolworths Mall.

THE TRIANGLE 1929

READING Cooperative Society opened its department store in Cheapside in 1928. Its functional style contrasts with the early Edwardian exuberance of McIlroy's store at the other end of the street. In the centre, behind the finger post, was the Palace Theatre, demolished in 1961, and on the right the former offices of Reading Board of Guardians and a Primitive Methodist chapel.

THE TRIANGLE 1986

A BUSY roundabout now links this end of town with the Inner Distribution Road. The Odeon Cinema opened in 1937 is on the right. The Coop was renamed Living in 1985.

STATION SQUARE
c. 1903

THE STATUE of Edward VII was unveiled on 3 December 1902. It was presented to the town by Martin John Sutton, of Sutton's Seeds, and the sculptor was George Wade. The Great Western Hotel behind it was opened in 1844, four years after the railway came to Reading.

STATION SQUARE 1986

TODAY THE statue stands on a traffic island planted with flowers. The Great Western Hotel closed in 1973 but this pleasing Italianate building was saved from demolition and is now used as offices. On the left is the Berkshire Athenaeum Club.

ST MARY'S BUTTS c. 1932

THIS BLOCK of shops obstructed the western side of St Mary's Butts and was demolished for road widening in 1932. Holmes the furnishers, who had had premises in the Butts since the 1860s, are here seen offering wonderful bargains in their clearance sale.

ST MARY'S BUTTS 1986

HOLMES WAS rebuilt in the Butts after the road widening but was again sentenced to demolition when the huge undercover Butts Shopping Centre was built and opened in 1972. This time Holmes moved right away to Chatham Street.

ST MARY'S BUTTS c. 1886

A GLIMPSE of very old Reading disappearing, showing a demolition gang at work (with spectators) 100 years ago. These brick almshouses backing onto St Mary's churchyard, had provided a last home for hundreds of poor old men and women. The plaque on the wall of those on the left read 'Founded by John Webb for four women 1653. Rebuilt by the Corporation 1790'.

ST MARY'S BUTTS 1986

THE REMOVAL of the almshouses was part of a plan to clear away insanitary buildings and open up the entrance to the church. The churchyard is now a pleasant green space and there are unobstructed views of St Mary's with its fine chequered tower.

CASTLE STREET c. 1883

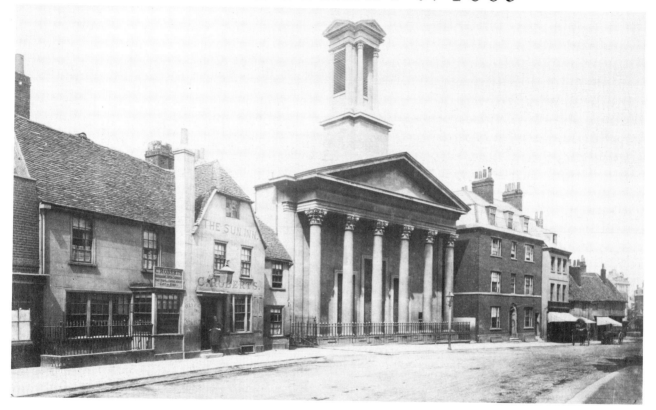

ONE OF the oldest inns in Reading, the Sun served travellers for centuries and here still advertises 'Broughams, open carriages, pony traps and saddle horses for hire'. Its extensive underground stables were occasionally used to accommodate circus elephants. St Mary's Chapel, built in 1798, replaced the original Reading Gaol, and is seen here with the classical portico and bell turret added in 1840–2.

CASTLE STREET 1986

THE TURRET had to be taken down for safety reasons about 1960. The Sun, smartly redecorated, still flourishes although beyond it, to the left, all this side of old Castle Street has been demolished.

SOUTHAMPTON STREET c. 1898

A VIEW seen by thousands of travellers entering Reading from the south as the road ran downhill to cross the Kennet streams. Small houses and shops faced the soaring spire of St Giles', added when the church was enlarged in the 1870s.

SOUTHAMPTON STREET 1986

TODAY one-way traffic, directed by overhead signs, rushes down to divide at a roundabout where the lower part of the street has been cleared away and a huge flyover is being constructed to carry the Inner Distribution Road.

WHITLEY PUMP c. 1920

THIS LANDMARK at the top of Whitley Street where it meets Christchurch Road and Basingstoke Road had been there since at least 1853. It provided drinking water for thirsty humans and animals, while the trees encircled by iron seats offered a shady oasis on a hot day.

WHITLEY STREET 1986

THE PUMP and seats disappeared several years ago when the present traffic island was constructed.

OXFORD STREET 1884

THE BEGINNING of Oxford Road was officially named Oxford Street until about 1887. On the left in the distance can be seen the Oxford Street Grocery Stores and, opposite, the Oxford Street Cafe. On the corner (left) was the White Hart, demolished and rebuilt during road widening in 1932, and (right) the Fox which closed in 1914 and was replaced by the Maypole Dairy until 1939.

OXFORD ROAD 1986

THE ROAD is wider and straighter now, with the Butts Shopping Centre on the left. The Maypole Dairy Corner has been occupied by shoe shops for over 40 years.

TIBBLE'S Model Bakery at 76 Oxford Road, on the eastern corner of Alfred Street. The bakery was behind the shop and behind the bakery were the stables for the delivery van horses – a convenient arrangement which would hardly meet with the approval of a modern health inspector.

TIBBLE'S Bakery was swept away along with other buildings in Oxford Road when the Inner Distribution Road was begun in the 1960s. Only the western side of Alfred Street (see here) survives.

A TYPICAL example of a popular corner shop in west Reading. Blundell's, as can plainly be seen, sold just about everything. In this photograph the proprietor and no less than eight assistants (not forgetting the dog) are lined up outside.

THE SHOP still stands on the corner of Gower Street and looks very much the same, although it has changed hands several times and is now Williams' general stores.

THE POND HOUSE was so named because, until the late 19th century, there was a pond on the opposite side of the road. By the time this picture was taken the pond had long been filled in and the electric tramways, opened in 1903, were in operation. Car no. 23 is about to make the return journey to London Road.

POND HOUSE was being redecorated when this photograph was taken. The buildings on either side are unchanged, retaining their original patterned brickwork.

THE PULSOMETER Engineering Company's works were built on what was then the edge of the town. Beyond it were open fields.

MODERN extensions have been added to the original works, now belonging to Sigmund Pulsometer Pumps Ltd. Since the borough boundary extension of 1911, Oxford Road has been built up more than a mile farther westwards.

THE ROEBUCK c. 1890

THE ROEBUCK was truly in the country in those days, and after Tilehurst Station was opened in 1882 it became a popular resort for boating and fishing parties. The back of the hotel enjoys views and access down to the Thames.

THE ROEBUCK 1986

TODAY THE Roebuck is the first building inside the Reading borough boundary along Oxford Road. The thatched building on the left in the earlier picture, offering ginger beer and cider to cyclists parched by the dust on the road, has been replaced by a brick extension.

SOUTHCOTE MANOR HOUSE c. 1920

ALTHOUGH considerably altered, this historic house dated back to the 15th century and was surrounded by a moat fed from the Holy Brook. The house and other buildings inside the moat were demolished in 1921.

SOUTHCOTE HOUSING ESTATE 1986

IN THE 1950s the Borough Council began to build a large housing estate in Southcote. By 1965 new streets had extended to the manor house site and the remains of the moat were filled in. The house stood at what is now the junction of Hatford Road and Circuit Lane, opposite Sheppley Drive.

WHITEKNIGHTS PARK 1927

SKATERS enjoying traditional Christmas weather on Whiteknights Lake on 20 December 1927. The bridge dated back to the 18th century when the park was a large private estate.

WHITEKNIGHTS PARK 1986

IN 1947 the University of Reading purchased Whiteknights, and campus buildings now fill much of the park. However the beautiful lake has survived, although the old bridge collapsed and has been replaced by one of modern design.

KINGS ROAD 1927

CHRISTMAS DAY 1927. Kings Road, deep in snow, is almost deserted except for a tram receding into the distance. The trees overhanging the railings screened early 19th century residences for professional men.

SOME OF THE houses on the left have been restored as flats and offices. Further along on the same side is Reading College of Technology. Railings, tram standards, gas lamps and many trees have gone.

CEMETERY JUNCTION c. 1955

THIS BUSY crossing of the London and Wokingham roads takes its name from the adjacent cemetery opened in 1843. In this picture a single policeman in the traffic control box is seen directing converging streams of goods vehicles. There are few cars in sight, and he obviously travels by bicycle.

CEMETERY JUNCTION 1986

THE LAYOUT of this junction has been greatly altered and traffic is now controlled by several sets of lights. Noticeably missing are the overhead cables of the trolleybus era.

FACTORY BRIDGE 1926

EXCITED crowds line Factory Bridge to welcome the Prince of Wales during his visit to Reading on 25 May 1926. In the background is part of Kennetside including the Young Prince public house.

KINGS BRIDGE 1986

IN 1937 Factory Bridge, so named because of its proximity to the famous factory which employed so many people, was rebuilt and renamed Kings Bridge in honour of the coronation that year of George VI. Kennetside, too, has changed in recent years.

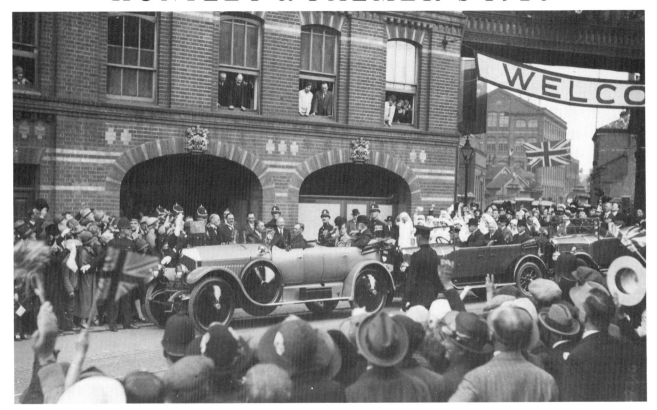

THE PRINCE OF WALES arriving for his tour of the biscuit factory on 25 May 1926. Huntley & Palmer's had been entitled to display the Royal Arms since 1867 when they were appointed suppliers to Queen Victoria. Factory workers in white overalls are among the welcoming crowds.

HUNTLEY & PALMER'S administrative offices in Kings Road were rebuilt in 1936 but biscuits ceased to be made in Reading in 1977 and all the factory buildings behind the offices have been demolished.

FROM CAVERSHAM BRIDGE c. 1898

BELOW St Peter's tower can be seen part of the Old Rectory, at that time a private house belonging to the Simonds family. In the foreground stand the timber frames which held baskets for trapping eels, then common in the Thames. Flowering rushes and other water plants grow in profusion.

THE EEL BASKET frames were removed in 1911. The Old Rectory, later known as Caversham Court, was demolished in the 1930s, although the gardens with their lawns sloping down to the river, are now open to the public. Trees have grown, hiding the church.

BONA'S BOATHOUSE 1890

THE Caversham Bridge Hotel was known at this period as Bona's. Antonio Bona also owned the boathouse (right), a fashionable place for hiring steam launches, house boats, punts and canoes.

THAMESIDE PROMENADE 1986

THE CAVERSHAM BRIDGE HOTEL was very badly damaged by fire in August 1986, soon after this picture was taken. Many of the pleasant trees have been cut down and the picturesque boathouse on the right has been demolished, which just shows how difficult it is to keep up with ever-changing Reading.

CAVERSHAM BRIDGE 1890

A VIEW OF the river bank at Reading approaching Caversham Bridge. Cattle graze in the field on the left. Just to the right of the distant church can be seen the three-storey ferryman's cottage which was moved in one piece eight feet from its original position during the building of the iron bridge in 1868–9.

CAVERSHAM BRIDGE 1986

THE PRESENT Caversham Bridge replaced the iron one in 1926. The rural character of this part of the river bank has disappeared.

THE THAMES 1926

SOME OF the industrial development at Reading which earned the town a bad name among lovers of the Thames. The crowds along the banks are watching the Prince of Wales arriving by launch at Reading Bridge during his visit on 25 May 1926.

THE THAMES 1986

IN THE 1970s the Reading Waterways Group prepared a report on the unlovely state of the Thames and Kennet through Reading, and since then efforts have been made to clean up the environment. The smoking chimney at least has gone.

GOSBROOK ROAD 1947

GOSBROOK ROAD links upper Caversham around St Peter's Church with lower Caversham which grew up round the mill. Here it is seen during the devastating floods of March 1947.

GOSBROOK ROAD 1986

HOUSES AND trees on the right have survived, but on the left there are now new flats and maisonettes.

CAVERSHAM WAR MEMORIAL 1928

THIS MEMORIAL to the 215 Caversham men who died in the Great War was unveiled on 5 May 1928 by Brigadier-General A. J. F. Eden, for many years a resident of Caversham. It was designed by Mr W. Hamilton of Priest Hill, Caversham, and erected by Wheeler Bros the local builders.

CAVERSHAM WAR MEMORIAL 1986

THE MEMORIAL can still be seen in Christchurch Meadows, although Caversham Bridge is now obscured by trees.

ACKNOWLEDGEMENT

All the old photographs in this book belong to the illustrations collection in the Berkshire County Local Studies Library, and have been reproduced by kind permission of the County Librarian.

The County Local Studies Library, based at the Central Library in Abbey Square, Reading, maintains a large collection of old photographs and postcards of places in Berkshire. If you have items relevant to any town, village or particular event in the county, the library service is always willing to accept donations for inclusion in its stock. The library also collects maps, prints, books and press articles about Berkshire, and a wide range of other items.

We would be pleased to discuss the origin or identification of photographs and postcards. To do so please contact the County Local Studies Librarian, Reading Central Library, Abbey Square, Reading RG1 3BQ. Telephone Reading (0734) 509243.

For a complete list of other Berkshire titles available from Countryside Books please write to:
Countryside Books
3 Catherine Road
Newbury
RG14 7NA